MY ACHING HEART

Edited by

Heather Killingray

First published in Great Britain in 2002 by
POETRY NOW
Remus House,
Coltsfoot Drive,
Peterborough, PE2 9JX
Telephone (01733) 898101
Fax (01733) 313524

HB ISBN 0 75432 742 6
SB ISBN 0 75432 743 4

FOREWORD

Although we are a nation of poets we are accused of not reading poetry, or buying poetry books. After many years of listening to the incessant gripes of poetry publishers, I can only assume that the books they publish, in general, are books that most people do not want to read.

Poetry should not be obscure, introverted, and as cryptic as a crossword puzzle: it is the poet's duty to reach out and embrace the world.

The world owes the poet nothing and we should not be expected to dig and delve into a rambling discourse searching for some inner meaning.

The reason we write poetry (and almost all of us do) is because we want to communicate: an ideal; an idea; or a specific feeling. Poetry is as essential in communication, as a letter; a radio; a telephone, and the main criterion for selecting the poems in this anthology is very simple: they communicate.

CONTENTS

THE JOKE

There was such an explosion of joy!
A dart of love employed
To a soft-red enduring place;
An exquisite smile released
Swirling atoms from their peace
And bright metallic things then
Gleamed onto a love-knot-ring.
Faded and came, faded and came,
Eyes blinked! To see initials there.
Glitters a blank space, a horrid place!
None to see? No reality? Just dreams.
Eros laughed at his painful prank
And I gazed at you across the lamp
The dart of love had lied, then died.

L P P

VALENTINE REPLY

The written message
Of your love beguiled,
And for a moment I forgot
Our arguments and tears . . .

I only remember when
We promised one another
With glad smiles,
And for a moment we forgot
Our pain, our doubt
And all our lonely fears . . .

For some there were - who
Mixed - faith love reviled:

Then, for-a-moment, I could not
Forget the bitterest years.

Delia Marheineke

BETWEEN THE TWO OF THEM

I have to choose between the two of them,
But my love for them seems unending.
Choosing just one of them means losing the other,
Forgetting half my love.
Sharing my love between them is tearing me apart,
But giving both of them up would break my heart.
One of them knows of my love,
Whereas the other is blind to my affections.
To know how each felt towards me would help my heart decide,
But love keeps me from even guessing what they ponder about,
It just makes me wonder even more.
One is a gentleman, the other is always there for me,
How many comparisons I make between the two of them forever.
After that second splitting my love would be like living two lives,
Both of which will be lies to my heart as I can't love both.
Until that time comes both will be as precious to me as there other.
I will love both even if it means tearing myself between the
two of them.

Samantha Olive

ANT AND CLEO

It was Ant's number on the display
As Cleo answered her mobile.
'Oh dear,' she sighed
And fluttered her eyes.
'I do hope he's not going to be vile.'

'Where are you?' he shouted
Down the phone
The line crackled and fizzled.
'I'm standing here in Actium
Solo, on my tod, all alone.'

'This is not what we discussed.
My Army is feeling pretty daft.'
'Hello, hello,' Cleo said
'This is a terrible line Ant dear.'
'*And I don't take kindly to looking like a prat.*'

Cleo, languishing in her bath
Gazed at her silky smooth legs.
She smiled with satisfaction
Her left hand held up to the light
The nails so shiny and red.

'Don't get in such a strop,
Ant dear.
After all I am the Queen of Egypt.
I have important business
I thought I made that clear.'

'Your fax said you were setting off
We were here all ready and waiting.
What could be so important?'
'Well, er, my acrylics had to be redone
And my bikini line needed waxing!'

Grace Green

RIDDLE OF LOVE

What is found when you're not looking?
Upon heart and mind it has a hooking,
Warm at first it seems to be,
Then cold, all turns like icy seas.
Playing upon mankind,
Tricks working full-time.
Yet here and there it can be tender,
Yoking those who's cares, they render.
Have you guessed this two-edged plight?
Whom on Earth's people it takes full flight,
An evil crow, a pure white dove.
Why of course, it is *love!*

F Divall

WHERE ARE YOU?

Where are you now?
What are you thinking?
What are you doing?

Wild imaginings embrace my mind
Cling to the subtle film of memory,
And I wander
Through the portals of the past
To the present and back again.

What are you thinking?
What are you doing?
Where, Oh where *are* you?

Flashes of light
Deepen memories.

With passion, I cling to the thin film.
Is it to be?

If only I knew
What and where you are now.

But I do know . . .

You are stroking my heart
With my mind.

Efua Abbam

TOGETHER

Relationships, are like walking a very straight line.
A tightrope, just comes to mind.
It starts off as taut, and controlled as I thought,
Then come to the middle, it's fraught.

It wobbles to the left then to the right.
While trying to work out true plight,
The only way forward, there's only one way
Letting each one have their say.

Keep focused in front to the goal at the end.
When each one of you learn how to bend.
Then look to the future, and say
We made it; everything is *our* way.

June Chorlton

STAR-CROSSED LOVE

Food, a glory from God indeed,
It lends to life the beauty of a bead.
Ill health often denies us of this precious gift
No chocolate, no pizzas to give us a lift.

A star-crossed love when food meets man
A star-crossed love, a definite ban.
Romeo and Juliet each other denied
No chocolate, no pizzas, oh no the reply.

A love affair with this wonderful food
Frequently now it's simply to brood.
Sickness comes if the law is broken
You can't even have a lick of the token.

Much thought is given to human love
But food is absolute when push comes to shove
My life of food enhances my ways
Its denial takes away the pleasure of days.

And so my lot is cast with those
Whose love they too could not choose.
A star-crossed love that goes amiss
And from the heart there flies a kiss.

Denise Shaw

REJECTED LOVE

Who reads the secret of a heart
That kept a flower by seasoned art.
Gently pressed upon a page
Speaks of love that touched another age.

These ageing pages now recast
A tender blossom blue
Both reflect upon the past.
And must resend my thoughts of you.

Just for a moment let me dream,
Across the age that lies between
To where your love its secret keep
A love still mourning as you sleep.

Your love nor mine cannot make
The years less bitter or forsake
A vacuum fills the vacant part
That cannot heal your broken heart.

Moistened by the dew of silent years
Cannot lighten or refrain
The stems of solace bind to these
The potent and the pain.

Love lies broken in the dower
Grafted by a tendril tie,
To leave behind a faded flower
That cannot be revived.

As the oyster mends the shell
Where once an ugly wound had fell.
Your love still speaks, this flower can tell
You bore a scar, and found no pearl.

T C Adams

IF ONLY

If only dreams and wishes came true.
If only you loved me the way that I love you.
If only I could go back in time;
To when I first met you.
If only I could change what went ahead.
If only life were so simple.
If only I didn't love you.

Rachel C Zaino

THE WEDDING VOWS

Deep cast shadows cross the rainbow's path,
where once stood a mountain, now a canyon lay
No heat to rise and radiate from the aged hearth,
No whispers in the night with the words you used to say
No arms embrace now when the troubles come
No one to worry when it's dark and I'm late home,
Folks change and you decided that our time was done.
So now I sit with memories and watch the telephone,
Will it ring today with the words I long to hear?
'I'm sorry darling, I was wrong, I love and miss you so.'
Why should it, as it's not just been one year,
But thirty-two since you decided it was time to go?
Why do I still wait? Watch phone and hunger for the postman's call?
Because it was a decision that you took upon your own
I still wander, desolate, up and down the empty hall
because I meant my vows and loved just you alone.
Sometimes at night I feel your breath upon my cheek
or hear your laughter from behind the door,
but though I quickly rise, a glimpse of you I seek,
I sadly return to bed aware you're not here anymore.
Imagination cuts my dreams of how things might have been.
resentment of the couples I see shopping, arm in arm.
But life itself, in reality, is no more than a dream,
And I have precious memories to keep me warm.
I want no other love, nor searched for one to take your place.
Reserved? Aloof? Perhaps, but time's not only on my side.
In reverie I smile as I still see your loving face
and note that it's not altered by passage of time and tide.
I have your youth encompassed deep within me
Whilst she sees thickening waist and the furrows of deep lines
so for her I surely feel no trace of envy.
For you were first, before she came, so very truly mine.

Channon Cornwallis

TO BE WITH YOU

When you walk in the room
My heart goes *boom boom!*
Couldn't stand the thought of you walking away,
It just needs to be clear
That my thoughts are sincere
And that I need you, both night and day.
If you feel like I feel
You'll know that it's real
And I'm here to show you the way.
Take my hand we'll fly high
Match our feelings in the sky
Come with me to the land of love
We'll escape
We'll go far
Where no one knows who we are.
Come with me to the land of love
This is our chance, now let's break free.
A new start for both you and me,
No more boundaries, no more tasks,
No one in the way now
Left to ask.
Come with me to the land of love,
Wherever you may go
Through rain, sleet or snow.
I'll be there for you
No matter what you do.
You're all I've ever wanted
And this much is true
The only thing I ever needed was
To be with you.

Terence Johnson

BROKEN PROMISED LAND

When you have reached the broken Promised Land
And dreams slip slowly through your hand
Life and love in a distance far
Wish upon a special star
With heavy heart your days seem long
New treasured love was like a song
But tender moments fall on stony ground
When deeds of pain utters no sound
Amidst the days of daily life
A journey of love to be a wife
Joys of laughter flitter away
To bring back the pain of yesterday
Once more to reach the broken Promised Land
Where dreams slip slowly through your hand
Tears fall silently from a heavy heart
Have we become worlds apart?
Can one return from the broken Promised Land
Where dreams slip slowly through your hand

Susan E Roffey

LOVE ETERNAL

My body sheltered the child we created
For nine long months, a time sadly fated
By the fortunes of war to spend far apart
The while she nestled beneath my heart,
A yearning within for the tender touch,
With closeness lovers have need of so much,
Flesh against flesh, feelings of bliss,
The senses astir from a soul-searching kiss,
Strong arms embracing in rapture untold,
Sweet moments denied to have and to hold.

But such not to be, even now down the years
I remember her birth, joy mingled with tears
Until across oceans you sailed with the tides
Love overflowing, arms enfolding, we cried.

Forty long years from that homecoming day
Abandoned once more, much further away,
Wallowing in sorrow completely forgot
The return of a dear one which thousands knew not,
Together so long as decades rolled by,
Nurturing memories that never will die,
A bonding forged which death does not sever,
Deep in a lonely heart it lives on forever.

Ellen Thompson

I LOVE YOU

When we fell in love on that fateful day,
I couldn't foresee the price I would have to pay.
I thought it was destiny: love from the start,
Never knowing one day you would break my heart.

The love we held was once so strong,
You said together is where we belong:
Walks in the moonlight, making love on the beach,
To the depths of my soul I thought you could reach.

I was in heaven right from the start,
But then you changed, and we drifted apart.
You had met another and just walked away;
I pleaded 'Don't go,' I begged you to stay.

I just want you back, I still love you so,
Turn around my love, stay and never go.
I love you so very much, words cannot say;
Just how much I miss you, be mine again, this I pray.

Maggy Copeland

IT GOES BACK IN TIME

Who went to Washington, I wonder who helped her to pay the
bill, that goes back a long way.
I am in black stockings, new at the Convent School and he at The
Christian Brothers, a smallish redhead with freckles on a bike
Who terrorised me by cycling too close to me and I too close to a
ditch on a 'sit up and beg' bike. I, with nose in the air, would not
look at either youths on their bikes, even though the darker
Adonis had just stolen the very first portion of my heart.
It's bald I'm told, the Adonis now, and I could pass him without
my awareness, the greatest love of my life, without his awareness.
The Brothers boys just stood in groups outside a draper's store to watch
the lovely Convent girls, in groups walk by, with their heads up
in the air, sideways a-glancing to catch his eye, so he does not
notice
these groups of youths were the pride of our land, some of them
knew and some of us didn't.
When the Convent doomed gate opened, bikes shot six to a
dozen, as the cars were few back then they had to look after
themselves, same applied to the Brothers.
On looking back we should have known it, we were a perfect
pack of males and females, just thinking and dreaming
what's under the rainbow.
The freckled redhead who terrorised me on the bike, is the one
who helped to pay my fare, the other an old dancing partner.
Not forgetting Sister Evelyn Chen, who was the perfect student
nurse, she paid for my grub, and I have lovely friends, I thank
all. Plus my family too, close and distant, (this is I who slightly mad).

Margaret Gleeson Spanos

TOGETHER FOREVER

He stood there so proud before the Queen Cleopatra
This strong handsome emissary from Rome
How his heart was beating as he looked upon her form
This beauty whose reputation was renowned

Never had he seen such darkened glowing skin
Or looked into two eyes of deep desire
Her smile had a welcome that melted his heart
And set his sleeping passion on fire

That evening they dined each a little afraid
Their destiny intertwined from that day
All of Rome and Egypt could never have foreseen
The great love that had been born so far away

Each night was spent together, pressed in each other's arms
Never caring what the future may bring or hold
But this was a love that never should have been
And Roman rule was always set in stone

How could he conquer the love of his life
And set his foreign flag upon her land
Rome was unforgiving to a rebel and his love
And sent its greatest army with high demands

Soon the battle of all battles raged upon the shore
Mark Anthony fought bravely for his Queen
But mortally wounded the last words from his lips
Were to the love that he would no more see

He promised he would love her in this world and the next
Her heart just broke in two at her loss
So she took her life to always be with him
Never more to be apart, they paid the cost.

Gillian Mullett

No More

No more will we walk beneath the moon
In a golden vale
Or feel the breeze playing a merry tune
In the merry month of May
No more will I swim in the depths of your eyes
Or taste and kiss the rose of your lips
Except in the deep expanse of a dream
Where I will find the gateway
To my heaven
And love it seems
Will have no end.

David A Bray

TRAITOR

Through whispered tears of silence quiet,
And without you the sounds shall never come,
The sounds of joy and laughter -
The sound of you when you wake in the mornings.
Through angry words and shouts of pain,
I loved you still and it is a shame,
What became of the happy ones.
The ones who assumed it would never come.
But she came and she slept in my bed.
I hope you know this is on your head.
Words could never convey my feelings
As I watched your reflections from a gap in the door,
And the sounds you made
Shall be heard no more.

Cathryn Harman

ABELARD AND HELOISE

Beauty, youth and innocence, a blessed trinity
but change may transform the swain's amour
from love's captivation to a closer affinity
with the nectar-filled bait of a Venus fly-trap lure.

As Abelard who gave his heart to Heloise
struggling in a tragic spring-loaded snare
was forced to face the perceived verities
of Heloise's powerful uncle Canon Flaubert.

An aspirant to priestly favours
where celibacy was a simple fact,
could not indulge in the fleshly flavours
others tasted in their marriage pact.

Their secret wedding disclosed - she bore a son;
preferment would not now fall on Abelard.
In an act of selflessness Heloise became a nun
her lover, caught in a maelstrom of assumed discard,
faced retribution of the cruellest kind;
enforced emasculation by an avenging petard.
Love tragically betrayed, love's signature unsigned.

Only in death were they reunited
to lie at rest together many hundred years.
Love sickens so when unrequited;
this sorry story told is bathed in hot salt tears.

Norman Meadows

I CAN'T FORGET

I can't forget the night we met, the college ball,
a quickstep, then a waltz. Each dance was like a dream.
The lights went down. I held her close; and when
the music stopped, we shared her red umbrella,
as we ran across the car park in the pouring rain.
Next day we walked upon the heath. Beneath the mellow
richness of late summer sun, we wandered hand in hand.
I can't forget the softness of her skin, that first
uncertain kiss, the cooing of two soft grey doves.
Among the songbirds and the trees we fell in love.

Within a month our lives were torn apart. September 1939.
War broke out. A crowded troop ship bound for France,
her tiny figure, miles away, standing on the quay.
And then the noise of war. Long lines of heavy trucks.
The deafening roar of tanks. *You won't get killed.*
Exploding bombs and mortars. The crash of falling masonry.
Sometimes there was only silence, and the falling rain.
Images keep coming back, clothing soaked with blood,
comrades dying at my side, half-dead soldiers lying
on the ground, dismembered bodies buried in the mud.

They sent me home for Christmas. Just a bit of luck.
I walked the last half mile alone, whistling through the rain.
My kit bag weighed a ton, and rubbed against my neck.
I didn't care. It wasn't far, the last house on the left.
I can't remember what I did or what I said. I know
she must have been killed instantly. I can't forget
the piles of rubble, personal things, a doll, some clothes,
the writing in her diary smudged out by the rain.
I found her red umbrella lying in soft mud, the cloth
in shreds like fingers, clinging to its broken frame.

AKS Shaw

ANNIVERSARY MEMORIES
(Dedicated to my darling wife, Valerie May Watson)

Many happy wedding anniversaries I have shared with you
And here it is November the fourth and that makes twenty-two.
The years have simply flown, how quickly they have passed
But I think we always knew our love was meant to last.
The year was nineteen seventy-six, the day was sunny and warm
And that was the very day our great love was born.
I'll never really know why it took so long to meet,
But darling once we did, our lives became complete.
Many were the early problems that we had to weather
It was never easy, but we tackled them together.
We battled against adversity like times when money was short
Because we always knew happiness could never be bought.
So far we have come together, for true happiness to find
Now we are bound together with the loving ties that bind.
Many people yearn for riches, which dominates their life,
But I have all the treasure I need, my treasure is my wife.
For I could never wish for a better companion or friend
With whom to share the journey through to life's very end.

Frank Watson

LITTLE HOUSE

Oh, little house that was to house Terry and me,
Do you feel lonely without us tonight?
Do you regret
Or do you forget
All the happiness that we had in sight?

Oh, little house, have you found a new dream?
Do warm love and beauty shine from your door?
Do you peep
At the sleep
Of young lovers who say: 'This is all that we wanted and more'?

Oh, little house, do you know what you've missed?
Do you know what's been lost and has faded away?
Hope and a dream
Are not what they seem,
And the visions of night have all crumbled by day.

You were to keep us until we moved on:
Our castle, protection, our solace, our home;
Where we would find
All that was kind -
But, two lost people, we still are alone.

Oh, little house, it was never to be.
Everything's broken, smashed at our feet.
Out in the night
Without any light
We cry for the day that was tender and sweet.

Wendy Vidler

THE MOMENT

It seemed but a moment we shared our lives
The crest of a wave on passing tides
Two pebbles washed upon one shore
Sunkissed dewdrops at early dawn

Soaring high above the seas
Spirits drift on gentle breeze
Two raindrops shared a distant cloud
Flowers bloomed on rocky mound

Golden sunrays could not outshine
This moment that was yours and mine
Too soon, the moment came and passed
Snatched from our hands, slipped from our grasp

Crushed pebbles lay scattered on the sand
Discarded dreams in heaven's hands
Darkness engulfs the empty space
Now sadness fills this lonely place

One heart now lives in a far-off land
With other angels, as destiny had planned
The crescent wave, cascades to shore
Drifting alone, to join the tides once more.

Christina B Cox

THE SNARE

Too much to forgive lies between us,
Too much holds us too close to part,
Too many brave new beginnings,
Too many changes of heart.

Sometimes I can no longer see you,
For the most blinding tears are unshed,
Closing in all around, is the silence,
The most wounding words are unsaid.

And shall we emerge from the half-light?
Or must it persist to the last?
As the heroine smiles of the ghost-wife,
Evoke only pale thoughts of the past.

A weariness deadens all hope now,
Ahead not a glimmer appears,
Whilst around us, forlorn and forgotten,
The flotsam of too many years.

M Mettam

HELPING OTHERS

I can't sit down and watch TV
Without the tissues beside me

A comedy, a good film, a horrible news report
Tears flood down my face, it's such a terrible disgrace

I've such a soft heart that friends and family turn to me for advice
And I sit and chat and say it's like that

I hate what the world turned out to be
I would share my food, my carpet and items as well

Wash their faces, scrub their hair
And tell them I love them and you should too.

Jay

THE FLAME

Been ripped apart so many times,
the truth sounds like a lie.
Retreating to my darkened heart,
to force myself to cry.

Can't escape the feeling,
when we're touching skin to skin.
Draw you to my silken depth,
and watch the world begin.

Fading light and worries,
as the dark dissolves the light.
Touching deep within you,
as the dark absolves my sight.

The sweet caresses of my youth,
will stir me as I sleep.
Of haunted dreams and mingled breath,
your touch I wish to reap.

Tangled breath, entangled hearts,
the spark is set to flame.
I feel the drawing heat cross through,
igniting inner pain.

Julia Bowler

MY BEST FRIEND'S HUSBAND

I love my best friend's husband
I love him very much
I tried to ignore my feelings
But couldn't ignore his smile, his glance, his touch.

I love my best friend's husband
I love him with all my heart
We tried to hide our feelings
Now we are together, never to be apart
He's not my best friend's husband now
For he belongs to me
My best friend's broken-hearted now, which I know I'll never be.

I have a new best friend now
And I've tried hard not to see
The way they look at each other
How close they've come to be.

I never dreamed it would be me
Who would be the one who is broken-hearted
Now he has left me for my best friend
My days and nights are full of tears since we've parted.

Ruth Howard

WINTER WEEKEND

It may be many years 'til we meet again,
if ever
winter's sadness has its icy hands clasped
round the heart that once so longed
to give and to partake in family life,

it may be many years 'til we meet again,
the cold clutches of a thousand wounds,
turn all helpful eagerness and longing
to painful failure and useless crying
laughter lines turn to marks of misery,

it may be many years 'til we meet again
let me bury the dead hopes, torn heart
and still-born words into the grave of
might-have-beens, with saddest songs,
love is of all, the most painful illusion.

Monica Redhead

AS MOONBEAMS DANCE

The lake a-quiver as moonbeams dance
And shooting stars the night skies lance
Heaven's canopy, a star studded sky,
Lights the path for a girl and boy.

This summer's night two lovers stroll
As moonbeams embrace body and soul,
Beside the lake with wavelets bright
Alone at last this summer's night.

Mist scented airs caress the two,
As they lie entwined on summer's dew,
A fading moon looks down on the scene below
As the dawns first light begins to show.

The flat calm lake, bathed by a silver moon,
For two lovers alone, a night gone too soon
As they leave the night to greet the day,
They watch the moonbeams dance fade away.

G Wright

BLUNT

The mother never liked him,
Though the daughter loved him whole,
He turned, from the closed door,
Cut deep, to the soul.
As he walked along the road,
The emptiness residing,
His thoughts in senseless turmoil,
It seems he was deciding.
That girl was all his life,
Without her left deep pain,
Life felt so cold and hopeless,
With no fruits left to gain.
Feeling the tears burst over,
He cared not that he cried,
He couldn't hide the anguish,
The light inside him died.
The darkness blurred the mind,
His vision reached to black
And at this ebbing low,
There was no climbing back.
That moment there, he knew,
He'd seen her for the last,
And knew he would become
Treasured - in her past.
Stumbling blindly to the bridge,
In rain, wind, water flow,
The noise became his heart
Rushing away, down there below.
He felt blunt,
He jumped.

Jillian Shields

Too Soon

A year ago you said goodbye
Too soon my love, for love to die,
To soon Eternity - and so
Eternity 'til your 'Hello'

Twelve months ago was your farewell
Twelve months for me so near to Hell
A Hell for me that will not go
Until the heaven of your 'Hello'

Three hundred days now since we met
So many lost, so much regret -
That time itself cannot discern
How many more 'til your return

Ten thousand hours now since your voice
To hear it made my heart rejoice
But no rejoicing e'er for me
Until again your face I see

A million minutes without you
What can I say, what can I do
I can't go on if you I lack
Please, please my darling,
Please come back

Innumerable seconds dear
Eternity makes of a year
The year ago you said goodbye
Too soon my love, for love to die

John Malkin

WHERE BURNING SAPPHO SANG

Tragic Sappho so maligned
Condemned by many modern minds
Spoken of in derogation
Once the pride of an island nation.

Lesbos home to thee sweet muse
Suicide thou sadly chose
You wrote of tender erotic love
Of mortals and the Gods above.

Truly sensual thou were
They claim 'twas girls that you'd prefer
Yet to death you leapt for the love of a male
Or so it's related in one such tale.

Whatever the truth it was at cost
Your superb poetry now mostly lost
Burned those priceless words in spite
On a shameful hot Byzantine night.

Lesbos where burning Sappho sang
Was your love for girl and man?
Today the love of both is fine
Were you born before your time?

C O Burnell

STAR CROSSED LOVE
(Alex and Nicholas)

She travelled
Far to see her
Czar, a young man
Nicholas, a rising star.
She so young,
Alex by name
Headstrong by nature
Yet afraid of fame.
Together they made
A perfect pair,
So in love but
What time to share.
They could not feel
The hand of fate
Which later would
Destroy with hate.

Janet M Baird

LOVE OR TRIVIAL PURSUIT

I've only seen her at a distance
But I feel I must take this chance
Once I've met her and we've spoken
I'll give a rosebud as a token

And after making these advances
Shall I ask what are my chances?
Would things be a whole lot better
If I just posted a letter?

But hold on, little love-torn twit
This is now the tricky bit
What's her address and what's her name?
Who shall I ask? I'm going insane.

Sleepless nights, tossing and turning
Days filled with heartfelt yearning
Is this love or shameful passion?
Will one kiss be a lover's ration?

How do I start to break the ice
With one so beautiful and nice
My heart skips a beat, then who knows
Is this the time for a single rose.

Her skin is like porcelain - Dresden china
I'll hold her hand as I wine her and dine her
So many things to ask with caution
Compliments on her bodily proportions.

The food is good, the company fine
She's an angel, I'm on cloud nine!
She kissed my hand - gave it a tweek
Now I won't wash it for a week.

Stanley Swann

THE WHITE WITCH AND THE SAINTLY DAEMON

Quite misunderstood they were
but their hearts and minds were pure.
They bathed in streams and waterfalls
Where leaves filtered midday sun through the tallest forest trees
Hidden by fresh moist vegetation.

They liked to breath in mountain air
and absorb the scents of wild plants
that sing out sweetly for pollination.
The humming birds and tiny bees
fill the lover's hearts with winged vibration.

Demands from high said separate
but passion burned and stole some time.
A full moon rose and lit the lakes
And dewdrops on all leaves and petals.
They huddled up close and planned out of sight
with help from nature and imagination.

Their fingertips touched and their eyes said now
with the rising sun they would pierce their hearts and fly.
They would weep upon the poisoned lands of fading Mother Earth.
Each human heart they'd try to soak with caring, love and fortitude
to mend the spoils of all hands and start rejuvenation.

Maria

LOVE UNCONQUERED

I'll tell you a tale of love that was spurned,
Of a wine-press trod sadly alone.
Of a heart that was breaking for some small return
From the friends and the folk he had known.
Oh yes, friends he had, and some stayed by him too,
Though puzzled and let down and sad.
It seemed all his life he'd rebelled just to lose
The little success that he'd had.
But his love vanquished all, it was all that he had
And every last drop that he gave.
For folk such as me, ungrateful, untrue . . .
He knew 'twas love only could save.
But love rose again and conquered all pain.
In this lies our hope, you and me.
The one who forgives, who will love to the end,
Gives us strength to break chains, makes us free.

E Morris

EARLY MORN

Shall I compare thee to the early morn?
Thou art warmer and a lot more bright.
Harsh frosts do freeze the tiny rose thorn.
And the morning's sunrise is just like night.
Sometimes the morning comes far too soon,
And its coloured complexion truly dies.
The golden sunshine must give way to the moon.
But nature's course dims the rays that bathe thine eyes.
As time goes on the morning begins to fade,
And the glorious rays that shine on thy face.
Nature's ways must dim the morn that thou hast made,
But heaven's brightness sends us angelic grace.
So long as thee remains in they memory,
Your life-giving image will remain with me.

Stephen Tuffnell

AN AFFAIR TO REMEMBER

As hand in hand we walked
Your silence touched my heart
For deep inside, I knew
The time had come to part
Freeing your hand from mine
You seemed on edge, confused
Unable even then
To tell me, I'd been used
Somehow, while it lasted
The truth I could not see
You knew it too and yet
Kept up the fantasy!
There was no final kiss
And nothing more to say
Because you were not free
I made you walk away
After you left, it rained
I cried for me! And you!
And all the clouds above
Seemed to be crying too

Patricia Whittle

DREAMTIME

I met you in my dreamtime
And loved you more than life
The only thing I wanted
Was to be your wife

And so we did get married
And all of heaven's blue
Was with me as I learned to know
The secret part of you

Your satin back, your shoulders strong
Your eyes so very blue
Your nape of neck, your golden hair
And the secret part of you

The way you held me to your heart
Each time I loved anew
And hoped that we would never part
And I lost the secret part of you

Alas you left me eight years on
For a younger woman too
So now I'm not the only one
Who knows the secret part of you

Well, now it's been a long long time,
And I can hardly say
That after nearly thirty years
I miss you every day

But I still think about you
And what might have been
If you and I had stayed as one . . .
Oh, the years in-between . . .

Diana Price

OSCAR WILDE

You are the prince of talent
Your spirit remains
I love your truthfulness
Does it matter what people think of you?
You are the angel of love
Hide your tears Oscar
For you and I, Bosie, are *one!*

Rajeev Bhargava

EXPERIMENTS
(To R)

They met through a friend
And knew where it would end.
His friends became hers
Who shared things about him that she loved to hear.
They all went out together, playing music, drinking beer.
In the back of the car she cradled his head
And he said:
'They told me not to mess this one up.
They told me to keep it good.
I don't want it to go the way of the rest.
I've been given a new chance to make this the best.
Please say nothing's gone wrong.
I so want to know nothing's gone wrong.
They told me . . .'

Sometimes they'd just stay at home.
Him and her, together, alone.
Cuddled and talked
Talking dirty, talking secrets, growing close soon.
Making love in the bathroom, playing games in his room.
They were happy together, doing the mundane.
But somehow she knew it would not stay the same.
Friends came between them, their own problems and pain.
When they parted she wished she could cradle his head
As he said:
'They told me not to mess this one up.
They told me to keep it good.
But now it has gone the way of the rest.
We've blown our chance to make this one the best.
I wish that nothing had gone wrong.
If only I could say nothing had gone wrong.'

Leanne Thompson

BRIDGING THE GAP

It's 'love that makes the world go round'
That's what people always say,
Well, I know that when I fell in love
We both had hell to pay!
It was back in nineteen sixty-two
The year I met my fate,
We were of different religions
So our problems were really great.
As a Catholic I was supposed to meet
And marry someone of the same faith too,
My church was really disapproving
So what were we to do?
Our parents were dead set against us
My mother tried every *'trick in the book'*
We were not welcome in each other's houses
But being in love all these insults we took.
In fact it just made us more *determined*
So often we'd to meet secretly
It wasn't romantic or exciting
We were both caused a lot of heartbreak you see.
We got a dispensation from my church to marry
And I stood outside the altar in tears.
As there were *no candles, no organ, no flowers.*
I regretted this treatment for years,
We've been married for nearly thirty-four years now
And I'd do the same thing all over again
But the rules have all changed and relaxed now
So the gap can be bridged with no pain.

Mary Anne Scott

PARTHENON BLUE

In the dimly lit hospital basement
the lagged pipes gently hissing,
a cockroach lies dead on the floor.
Two nurses come together, starched white hats
bob closer. A secret whispers between them.
'Doctor M is taking someone to Athens.'
The pipes sigh in realisation,
'It's you isn't it? It's you.' The cockroach trembles.
And suddenly the Parthenon stands before us,
in all its glory against a sky of impossible blue.
Three days to understand this civilisation.
We throw our arms around ancient pillars.
We stumble over the ruins of Corinth.
We gaze deep, deep down into the Canal.
We laugh together at the cabaret
in the night-club under the Acropolis
where the jokes are in Greek but
we understand them and each other.
Your slender fingers that sew hearts together
feed me with apple slices soaked in wine.
Tiny specks of blood on your glasses remind me
of the times away from this magic. No matter.
I see myself in the cracked and dusty mirror
a face so full of happiness the sky is within it.
The spells of this ancient world do not last,
the blue is diluted to grey and tears.
I hope you are sewing hearts in South America.
I would have followed you there or anywhere.
Instead I remember the blue and the secrets
whispered in the basement.

Elizabeth Rigby

HEART ECHO ... ECHO ...

An echo through the air
Through the night
In the valley
From the mountain
to the alley
Where it echoes
in the light
On the crowd
As they wait . . .
In the silence
At the gate . . .
For the grinding of the
Pithead wheel to
Echo . . .

echo . . .

ec . . .

Carolyn Smith

UNTITLED
(To a special friend)

My heart is crushed
Because of my cowardliness
My heart is placed in one piece
Because of your compassion
Whether you are there or not
Your beauty seems to dwell
Just a thought about you
Makes my fragile heart swell
There's a burning heat
That scalds my inside
It will be there forever
As long as you put me aside
Wherever I run to
You always seem to be there
There is a reflection of you
That makes me want to stare
My heart is suffering my aches
I don't know what it's from
It makes me think of you
Especially now you're gone.

Duncan James Roberts

MY STAR CROSSED LOVE

I have love fixations for my lover Bluebeard for aeons
If my darling thrush could carry me to him tonight
Oh how the flames of deep love and passion would rise in my soul
Miles and space have divided me Augusta from my tender
loving Bluebeard
I dream about him, I think about him daily
Surges of great desire well up in my heart
All is hopelessly in vain
The darkness enters
Like as if I was riding a bicycle on a lonely stretch of country road
Without a flashlight
And suddenly get a puncture
And have to laboriously trek the miles alone unaided
A holy terror and two frets
Is the deep pain gilded within my soul
My tears flow that could cause a spillage of the Pacific Ocean
I thump myself with leaden blows
And I remain motionless on the roadside until the break of day
Is lost love worthy of such pain and heartache we'll see . . .

Rita Cleary

LA PRINCESSE DE CLÈVES

Passion is a long, slow sickness
For which there is no cure,
And I, I am weary, weary unto death,
Of an old, old passion.

Love unborn can never die.
Love untendered cannot be withheld.
Love undeclared cannot confound in the utterance.
Love in the embryo aborted can neither wither
Nor grow stale in the maturing.
Love unsanctioned and impossible -
Witness the love of Tristram for his Iseult,
Of Lancelot for Guinevere -
Rings, in despite, prodigious, down the centuries.
Love unfulfilled for ever, must surely be eternal.

Is it not so, my love? Oh, say that it is so.
Alas, it is not so.

For love unborn forms icicles around the heart.
Love undeclared strangles the living breath,
Murders the babe, untenderly.
Unsanctioned love offends the sight of God,
Whose eye abortion stabs.
And love unrealised is utter unfulfilment,
Nothing more, for ever.

Neither in sophistry nor casuistry is comfort.
Oh, my illicit love, there is no comfort anywhere.

Passion is a long, slow sickness
For which there is no cure.
And I, I am weary, even unto death,
Of an old, old passion, for which there is no cure,
Only extinction.

Faith Bissett

WHEN TED MET SYLVIA

Sparks flew when the man from Yorkshire moors
met the love-bite girl from Boston

magnetic attraction
iron filings of poems

locked into bondage
of words on paper

her inside herself
him outdoors in nature's way

her clear New England voice
faltering in damp Devon

his strength demanded
new challenges

two planets in different orbits
distant as Venus from Mars

passion dampened,
poetry exploded.

When Ted left Sylvia
frayed by her inner turmoils,

poems flew from her pen like startled birds,
prompted by unseen dangers,

stabbed birds in pain
cold from the dark

her flame and spirit
left in ashen words

his vigour, in lines
of timeless insight

Marian Reid

THE STONY PATH

There was a little girl
Who went for a walk in the woods
And strayed from the stony path.
She found a timbered hut
And knocked on the knotted door.
There stood a blind, old man
Dressed in strange, runic robes.
He beckoned her to sit on the floor
Softened with a Turkish, tasselled rug.
With a palmistry of withered fingers
Threading alien prayers and impostors on to a Rosary,
He folded his sorcery around her.
She levitated above dusty, papyri scrolls
And pagan parchments
And flew.
She flew and her eyes were livid coals
And sparkled with a predatory vision.

He saw the bazaars of Babylon
Where his empire had been raised by guile,
The minarets of Persian realms,
The shores of Marmaris where he learned to dream.
He remembered being plagued by the
Vagabonds of the Hellespont.

She followed spice routes,
And trade winds swept her to
Hover over tamarind trees near
The Isthmus.

He saw the two lovers under the stars
And he remembered the girl who taught
Him to forget all the languages of youth.
Their voices rose echoing
From luminous shells that glittered

In the density of earth's lost surfaces.
Nights were fat and slothful and they coiled
Like a serpent on the sentient sea that sloughed its skin to the
Rhythms of the planets heavenly song.
But her eyes turned elsewhere.
He gouged his eyes.

The leathery, purple gaze, bid her return
And softly she hushed down on the wooden floor,
Tassels stilled
Wind silent.
Her eyes were still strangely glittering
Fuelled by an archive of personal reliquary
That burned deep within his soul.
She might come back to the woods one day
And once again stray from the stony path.
She might.
One day.

Robert Vizard

GOOD FOR HER!

I don't know why our common comrades
insist on updating me
with your current status -
each misfortune.
Every titbit of happy news.

They must know - it had oft been displayed
for any and all to see -
my love is a lattice
a vast compound
of emotions founded around you.

It must show (*must*) that I am dismayed
by your absence, never free
of memories; that is
never immune
to each torment you endure, each bruise,

each joy. Yet that litany's replayed
over and over . . . frailly -
waif of phrase once fat as
a pig - dry tune
of 'Good for her!' Shredding soul anew.

Perry McDaid

ROXANNE ET CYRANO

He Cyrano - yearns to revere
How much he loved - adored her
Poet, theatre critic - master swordsman
He of the rapier-like wit
How could she fancy him
With a nose such as his
Enter Christian -
Shy, handsome - but unable
To articulate, his feelings for Roxanne
He begged Cyrano - to put poetry into his mouth
So Cyrano - expressed his love for Roxanne
Through Christian.
She was smitten - thinking
The poetic sentiments were Christians
Take care of Christian in the war
She beseeched Cyrano
Sorrow deep in his heart, he agreed
Knowing she had fallen for his words
Expressed by another
In the heat of battle, unable to keep
His promise - Christian was killed.
Heartbroken, Roxanne fled to a nunnery
Alone, with her grief
Alleviated only by visits - by Cyrano
One day - late for his visit
Betrayed by enemies - ambushed
Dying - he struggled to keep his appointment
Finally dying in her arms - repeating words of love
She'd heard before - too late, she realised
It was Cyrano - not Christian, the words belonged to.

Rod Palmer

GOODBYE MY LOVE
(Writing as Abigail Williams for John Proctor,
The Crucible by Arthur Miller)

As I look into the twilight sky, a cold wind gushes past
The moon casts shadows on the water, as if lighting my path.

Dreams I once had, can no longer be
Dreams of passion and love, now an endless sea.

If only life was a dream. A dream that never ends
How full my life would be, the love that I could send.

I've left that love behind, the times that we have shared
If only we were together, if only I had cared.

The memories I have taken, the passion in my eyes
Let love flow down my cheeks, let you hear the love I cry.

I sail on this boat, stars shining above
Dreaming what could have been, dreaming of my love.

Time is an anchor deep beneath my heart
I will never forget this love even when apart.

This is the beginning these times past and gone
One day we will be together, together again as one.

We will meet again someday upon the wings of love
Sweeping us up to Heaven, up, up way above.

Our love is pure and deep, deep within our hearts
Our hearts will join together, never to be apart.

My love for you is true I will wait until the end
Waiting here forever, our love will never bend.

Now I say goodbye to a love that is true
Remember in your heart that I will always love you

Lindsey Knowles

THE MEETING BETWEEN OTHELLO AND DESDEMONA

Like a ripe fruit thee revealed thyself;
An Act of God.

I was alone with thee,
Quaking like a leaf,
Innocent.
Neither realising,
That we might ever enter feeling,
Deep within God.

Elizabeth Rose French

The Ice Well

I put my first rose in the ice well
        Deep, deep,
It will always be there
To show that I care.

I took my first kiss to the ice well
        Keep, keep,
Forever in truth
The freshness of youth.

I gave my fierce pain to the ice well
        Sleep, sleep,
In that cold oubliette
While I try to forget . . .

Margaret Clary

LINKS OF LOVE

How sweet the ties of love can be
When each of us loves firstly Thee,
Then puts the other first, before
Themselves, or any earthly store.
So deep this understanding plain,
Words, to describe it, try in vain.
We think and feel almost as one;
Have blending aims - when all is done.
We share our joys and share our woes
In prayer before our Lord, who knows.
Words are scare needed, each can share
The other's pleasure, feel their care.
I thank my Lord for a friend like you
Who weeps with me, laughs with me too.
This threefold cord can't broken be
While each of us is linked to Thee.

Mary Pledge

Eros In Flight

Cool - calm
The shuttered eyelids show
A swollen weeping,
And the racing glow
Is silent, sleeping.
Resigned in love
the recumbent form is stilled;
Discarded raiment
Minutes the body filled.

Yet is sensed a sadness in the pose.
Although the hand is closed
As if to stay his going,
Love goes.

Janine Vallor

LOVE IS A STRANGER

Love is a stranger,
Love is the strangest thing,
Love is the changer,
Love changes everything.
Let love change you,
Even though
You may not know
The answer,
For you will never
Be the same again,
Save for your name.
Let love reclaim you,
Even though
Love is a danger,
For you will come to know
The stranger,
In the darkened room
Is you.

Stewart Gordon

SOUTHERN PEARLS

Southern pearls are white, silvery spheres
appearing almost new, having a sapphire hue,
a golden glint, a ruby tint and just a hint
of emerald too!
Southern pearls - so solid, so smooth, possessing
an engaging presence that's lavished and
lacquered from a place of pleasance.
Southern pearls are treasures of sensual
substance, scarcely spread and sparely seen yet
sought in abundance.
Southern pearls enchant the feeling heart from
the encountered start, firing unrest amongst the
silently disconnected yet stirs interest with the
conversing connected . . . who want a second peep . . . thus
causing a yearning to caress and to keep.
Southern pearls being briefly mislaid means
precious attention is not being paid, thus the
aching absence saddens . . . then the reviving sense
of return gladdens when being right up front after
being left behind, dazzling the eyes and illuminating
the mind from past caring to future kind.
Southern pearls can be craved but not carved,
polished without reflecting the self image yet
prized without a projecting homage.
Southern pearls upon warm accommodation are proud
decoration for the full duration, to cherish with
the good and also the bad days . . . or perish always.

Simon King

BROKEN BOUGH OF BLOSSOM

The broken bough transfixed my eye,
As I was hurrying passing by,
I stopped to gaze . . . to weep unseen,
Sad at the beauty that had been.
Its leaves so fresh, so green a-strew
Its blossoms pink and red in hue.
Why should this tragedy take place?
And then therein I saw your face.

Yes, you too are broken now,
At the shattered wedding vow.
Your beauty bruised and crushed beneath
The promise he did not bequeath.
Broken bough, bruised blossoms in the dust,
Destroyed within the wild wind's lust,
Your leaves so green, your beauty not full grown,
Lascivious lapping of the wild wind's moan.

Broken love, lost, languished in the mire,
Betrayed by lustful lure of Man's desire.
Your trust so sure, your beauty not full grown,
The sobbing, throbbing of your heartbeat's moan.

Aleene Hatchard

LOOKING

How do we find what is lost?
Looking for eyes to believe in.
That familiar smile and face,
That same warmth and feeling.

Please tell me because I don't know.

Jamie Barnes

ENDYMION

Filmy in black lace, evening floated down,
Stirred, and headily swayed to husky whispers
From seductive night breeze. Velvet shadowed,
Her lawn glowed chiaroscuro through full haloed
Mists of gauzy moon inscrutable - Dietrich behind a veil.
A candle burned, flickered. Moon's warm lips smiled.
She watched her fawn descend into a torpid trance
While he gazed mesmerized across the hush of night
Where cannabis posed inside a window's single light.
She stroked his neck, rose, swept out from the gate
And passed among the groves through obscured vines
On pathways undergrown, closed, over stones to stony
Mausoleum, church, and quiet place, its yard new-mown,
And breathlessly paused to watch the mower of the lawn
Daub the sweat and moonlight blue that kissed his youth,
His moist skin's hue, as he rested on a marble chair.
She shuddered sighs, and rushing there, she nestled warmly
Next to him. *'The lawn's prepared,'* she said, *'but still*
Remains some mowing yet to do. I show the way and you
Shall follow me.' 'To finish work I've not begun!' laughed he.
'Venus loved Adonis. Please tell, I ask you, who are you?'
'I am not the pining love of Venus, the love Diana slew.'
Then rushing wind-clouds rustled now the groves and skies
And unveiled Diana glowed on him her vaselined bright eyes.

Edgar Wyatt Stephens

ALVIS

You really are an ugly boy, she said - meant it,
As her fingers touched so cruelly
The grotesque lines of my face,
A long nose, oily skin - damp and leathery.

Sickness prevailed within deep - how could she?
The dawn was still curtained, the world resting,
Yet I knew, she would be gone soon,
An hour, maybe two, when the day is young.

Alone, my only friend, the warmness of the bed,
Still fragrancy with sweet flowers.
The clenched pillows, still, wishing to be undisturbed.
Never to be told of her eternal absence.

Will I never again feel her touch,
Her breast pressed lovingly against mine?
Our hands entwined as lovers - arms serpentine,
Nimble and cold, clutching at straws.

The door closing silently, I raise with questioning vigour,
I see her back, no goodbye, no kiss, no dream
The footsteps on the stairs, the usher at the front door,
I close my eyes and wait for the dawn.

S P Springthorpe

BLEAK WEATHER

Dear Love, where the red lilies blossomed and grew
The white snows are falling;
And all through the woods where I wandered with you
The loud winds are calling;
And the robin that piped to us tune upon tune,
'Neath the oak you remember,
Over hilltop and forest has followed the June
And left us December.

He has left like a friend who is true in the sun
And false in the shadows;
He has found new delights in the land where he's gone,
Greener woodlands and meadows.
Let him go! What care we? Let the snow shroud the lea,
Let it drift on the heather;
We can sing through it all; I have you, you have me,
And we'll laugh at the weather.

The old year may die and a new year be born
That is bleaker and colder;
It cannot dismay us; we dare it, we scorn,
For our love makes us bolder.
Ah robin! Sing loud on your far distant lea,
You friend in fair weather!
But here is a song that's fuller of glee
By two warm hearts together.

M S Cornbill

THE CRUEL ARROW

The banquet was o'er and Aeneas began to recount the night so dire
When his homeland, the city of Troy, was reduced to ashes by
Greek fire;
As Queen Dido of Carthage clung on to his words, she felt Cupid's
arrow strike her.

Next morn Carthaginians and Trojans rode out for a hunt on the
African moor;
Aeneas' lad Ascanius was hoping to bag a lion or foaming boar.
Several miles from the palace the rain lashed down and the thunder
started to roar.

Nymphs shrieked on the mountain tops, lightning flashed; Aeneas and
Dido came,
As the fates had ordained it, down to a cave where, casting aside
all shame,
Their union took place: the queen called it marriage, concealing her
guilt in that name.

Through the wintry months in her new city of Carthage Queen Dido
cherished Aeneas;
She'd not known such love since the brutal murder back in Tyre of her
husband Sychaeus.
Her happiness, though, was not destined to last - in the gods' eyes
it was not felicitous.

One day the gods' messenger Mercury flew down and addressed
Aeneas in this way:
'You're wasting time here while a different land, decreed to you,
awaits your sway;
King Jupiter has sent me to warn you to set sail for Italy without delay!'

Dido soon knew the Trojans were planning to leave - such news could
not long be denied:
'So you hoped, did you, cruel Aeneas, to go without saying goodbye?'
she cried;
'It's blatantly obvious now that, whenever you said you loved me,
you lied!'

Aeneas, aghast, gave a harsh, curt reply: 'I owe you much, Dido,
it's true;
But Apollo of Grynium and Mercury himself have warned me - so
what can I do?
I must make a new home in Italy, that is my fate - and there's no place
for you.'

'You were not born of a goddess,' sobbed Dido, 'Hyrcanian tigresses
suckled you!
I rescued you when you were shipwrecked and starving, I cared for you
and your crew;
I foolishly gave you a share in my land, and now this is what you do!

If Apollo of Grynium and Mercury himself have warned you,
you'd better depart.
I just hope that out on the rocks in mid-ocean your ships will be
torn apart;
It would be an appropriate price to pay for so callously breaking
my heart.'

At sunrise next day the queen spotted the ships out at sea and could
bear it no longer:
She built a huge pyre and then threw herself on the sword which her
lover had given her.
Pious Aeneas from his boat saw the funereal smoke, but did not concern
himself further.

Ian Whalley

MY SOLITARY COMFORT

With your breath still warm inside my ear,
Closed eyes release just a solitary tear.
That weaves its way through my weary face,
Rolling slowly at first, then gathering pace.
It lingers at the corner of my mouth and then,
Like life's bitter ways, it carries on rolling again.
Clenched eyes will not see its marauding path,
The internal darkness seen, covers its aftermath.
Despite no audience it quickens it runs,
Onwards it spirals, waiting for others to come.
Slowly but surely its brothers appear,
Beautifully glistening each solitary tear.
As each one serenely passes by my lips,
They brush just slightly as if each were a kiss,
Silken-like placed by your angelic touch,
Warming me inside, it all seems too much.
And as two fuse to form just the one,
It's like we're together again, where all this began.
Yet you are no longer here, just waiting in the past,
And the realisation of this fear, has more tears to cast.
They join with their brethren, naked in the dark,
Flowing happily together, all leaving their mark.
Until they come to the first tear I shed,
To join forces, and roll onto my bed.
There they will wait, at their journey's end,
Each solitary tear, with the strength that I lend,
For them to appear each night whilst alone,
They comfort my nightly, for this I cannot condone
Their appearance, for I am weak without you here,
For you are each and every solitary tear.

Garon Coles

YOU WERE THERE

It is paved with the moss of virile rivers and chipped by a
                              chiselled wind,
that cobbled path all broken there and bared to the tangled weeds.
It gives its neck to the darkened step and the blistered door above,
then flakes away to a shaggy lawn which died 'neath the house of love.

* * * * *

I thought of the night and its languishing hour and my senses
                               extra keen,
but again and again o'er the water it came, low-pitched, pleading
                               and clear.
I shook with the ferns and deep undergrowth, I stood upright
                               peering there
for the plaintive cry unsettled me and my racing heart froze.
For there again the cry from out the mist was clear . . . Darling
                               I am here,
near the riverbank and our bridge. I could not move but faintly called.
I can't see you for the night, tho' moon had gleamed behind the
clouds when I arrived, 'twas now gone, vanished out of sight.

The echo of my failing voice lingered in the air, I called again, Ivan
                               I'm here,
I'm here, and saw the outline of our house; he was there, he was there.
Inside that ragged tomb he'd kept his vow knowing I would come again
along that wooden bridge to keep a tryst years ago we both had made.
And there he stood with arms outstretched, crushing me to death,
kissing years of tears away and lonely heartache.
Promising ne'er to leave again 'neath a canopy of stars, staring at my
streaming face . . . But now 'tis dawn I am alone, but with me remains,
The memory of that night and warmth of his passionate embrace.

Ann Safe

FEATHERED FRIENDS

My parents said, 'Oh no, my sweet,
You cannot wed a Parakeet.
You're young, and in good time we feel
You'll meet a handsome Cockatiel.'

I started then to plead and beg
But they told me that from an egg
They'd told me that my fate was sealed -
I'd have to wed a Cockatiel!

But oh, his feathers caught my eye,
And I shall love him 'til I die.
It really is not fair of fate
To make me have another mate.

I wanted us to fly away,
But then he told me he was gay.
So then I thought how quite absurd
To love a homosexual bird.

So now I sit alone and cry,
And watch the Parakeets fly by.
Who knows, one day I'll maybe feel
That I can love a Cockatiel . . .

Anne Rolf-Brooker

SHIVERS
(For Pat M - Now know as Mrs F)

You made shivers
Go down my back
Whenever we met
Talked
At bus stops
Or Woolworth's
The same old thing
Shivers
I don't think I ever kissed you!
Not even when I was drunk!
I met you
Years after
With your husband
And children
But the shivers
Had gone!

Paul Wilkins

MY SPECIAL LOVE

How well I remember the night we met
A time in my life I shall never forget.
My friend had arranged a 'blind date' for me
What would he be like - I thought and would he like me.

My friend and I used to go out once a week,
Thursday night was ladies' night so to speak.
The night when the women were loose on the town
In pubs and clubs by the dozens they could be found.

We sat in the pub drinking sweet white wine
Waiting for the hands on the clock to reach nine.
As the time came at last imagine my surprise
Someone I already knew stood there before my eyes.

'Long time no see,' was his greeting to me.
'Are you married? - I am - but not happily.'
'A divorce is on the cards as things didn't work out in the end,
The rows drove me up the wall and nearly sent me round the bend.'

'Can I take you home?' he asked. 'It's on my way.'
My friend had already left with her boyfriend it was the end of the day.
But he didn't drop me at the arranged place
Instead he drove on into the country with a smile on his face.

We made love that night which led to many times more,
A love which grew so special, I grew to worship and adore.
We had to go careful not to be seen,
When we were together it seemed like a dream.

Then the blow came he was being sent away
He would have to move with his firm - what could I say.
We tried to say goodbye as we clung to each other
I was sobbing hysterically as me in kisses he smothered.

My heart was broken - I loved him so much
That friendly smile and tender touch.
I still miss you my special love and always will too
And I know in my heart I will never forget you.

Marjorie Ridley

My Own Scottish Flower

My own Scottish Flower
She blooms but like no other
No flower in all the world
Could be nearer to my heart

I care so much about her
Though she may not be aware
I would give my life up for her
To think that she might care

She is a sweetness in the mornings
And a comfort to my soul
My heart is hers forever as I live
And yet grow old

In the evenings she is so fragrant
After dark she is so warm
I feel the warmth flow from her
As she comforts me till dawn

I tend her every evening and
Gently she responds
I am helpless in her presence
As she holds me in her arms

I could never find more happiness
If I had all such power as I have
Found in this my lifetime with
My lovely Scottish flower.

Linda my love, my life.

F J Lawton

MY HOLIDAY LAMENT

I followed walkers on the beach one day
The waves were rolling and covered in spray.
Footprints everywhere in the sand
I longed for you to be there to hold my hand.

The hotel we had stayed in could
Clearly be seen.
You were standing beside me, but
'Twas only a dream.

I stood and gazed at the roaring sea,
It almost seemed to beckon to me.
'Come in, come in,' it seemed to say.
'Come, drown your sorrows in my cool salt spray.'
Shall I take heed and go in I thought
The sand and sea so many memories had brought.

Should I go in and drown my sorrow?
No! Live to fight yet another tomorrow
And trust in God to bring you back
Into paradise where nothing will lack.

I had a deep yearning for you to be by my side
I know I have to come to terms with it
That really you have died.
I looked across at the purple hills,
Palm trees, different shades of green
I know I can now be happy,
To have been where you have been.

Jayne Pickard-Wood

THE LOVE OF MY LIFE

I felt an overwhelming love,
I'd met my prince in life,
My one and only ambition,
Was to be his loving wife.
I thought I had really loved before,
But nothing was quite like this,
Just being together all alone,
Was sheer and utter bliss.
I thought of the well-known lovers,
In history and of fame,
I realised this great passion,
Was very much the same.
I was really eager for his touch,
My body was like a fire,
This was entirely new to me,
Of his lovemaking I'd never tire.
The wedding dress was white satin,
With a long lacy kind of train,
I felt so wondrously happy,
My feelings I couldn't restrain.
Six months of total happiness,
Then all at once the shock,
A strange woman stood on the step,
My knees began to knock.
Does John Garfield live here?
I've reason to believe he does,
I want to know if this is true,
I don't want to make a fuss.
He's left something behind,
I thought I'd let you know
Just me and our three children,
I've been searching high and low.

My husband was a bigamist,
And now I'm all alone,
I've lonely years ahead of me,
In which I can atone!

Edith Antrobus

KING DAVID AND BATHSHEBA

King David was staying on Mount Zion.
One evening at sunset, he saw a beautiful
lady in the garden. Inquiring who she
was, a servant told him she was Bathsheba,
wife of Uriah an officer in the king's army.
David sent for Bathsheba,
fell in love with her, wished to
take her as another wife but
could not while Uriah was living.
David sent Uriah into the front line
of battle where there was no escape.
He was killed by the Ammonites.
David took Bathsheba into his palace.
She became his wife. In due time a
child was born. Few knew how
Uriah died but God knew and was
displeased. David was punished
The child of Bathsheba whom he loved
dearly died. Absolom the King's son
tried to take the Kingdom from his
father King David. Absolom trying to
escape in battle rode under an oak
tree and his great mass of long hair tangled
in the branches. Absolom was left hanging.
Joab pierced his heart with darts and
Absolom died. Another blow to King David
at the death of his favourite son.
The king betrayed Uriah a warrior who
was faithful to king and country.
God punished King David severely.

Francis Gibson

THE LOVE OF THE FATHER HEART OF GOD

Beyond the clouds, where Heaven's host do gather,
I peered into the distance with a searching spiritual eye.
The cumulus, like banks of foaming lather,
Rose up like pillars to support the framework of the sky.

The chariots of God, bathed in the glory of their Master,
Descended on the wings of the eternal cherubim,
Wheels within wheels spinning ever faster,
The glorious heavenly transport for Salvation's mighty King.

For Jesus Christ, the Holy One, in all His glory vested,
Moved through the galaxies towards the favoured time.
His beloved saints, on earth so grievously tested
Reached out to him in love to form an avenue divine.

As mighty angel forces appear above this planet Earth,
Something truly miraculous is going to take place.
The dynamism of Heaven is bringing into birth
A special brand of people, a superhuman race.

The world will seem to tremble at the thunder of the Lord.
Graves were rent asunder by Christ's resurrection power.
An explosion of the elements, through God's own living word,
For wonder of wonders, this is Redemption's hour.

Conscious of a new dimension then, and adorned in linen white,
Changed forever in a moment, in the twinkling of an eye,
A product of the grace of God, displayed in rainbow light,
The saints raised from mortality to eternal realms on high.

I H Davies

LOST AND FOUND

In my youth, I found God,
In adolescence, I lost God.
In medicine, I found God,
In philosophy, I lost God.
In living, I found God,
In explaining, I lost God.
In ordination, I found God,
In aridity, I lost God.
In prayer, I found God,
In complacency, I lost God.
In village homes, I found God,
In Church Councils, I lost God.
In serving Him, I found God,
In 'team ministry', I lost God.

Perhaps, if I live long enough,
I may, yet, find God,
Again,
For He ever sought me, far off,
And brought me home.

John Beazley

MORE LIKE LOSING GLASSES

It's not like losing money,
A watch, a bet,
Or losing your place in a book.
It's more like losing your specs.

A day can be lost,
Or time, or track.
There's losing your train of thought.
But, sadly, it isn't like any of that.

It's drifting first.
Then it's losing focus,
Then panicking in mist.

Love lost
Is lost sun,
Dew, morning coffee,
Drifting snow,
And private laughing.

Richard Moffatt

THE GREETING

Like thunder, echoing on canyon floor
In her resting place she hears his cry
Like the screaming eagles on pinnacles of stone
With wings at his heels

Like the raging wind he comes
As golden rays pierce through, the fortresses
As old as time
He comes

His scent is carried on silent breeze
With searching eyes she scans
She sees
He is near to her now

She calls
Urging him onward to her side
Like the arrow he flies straight and true
Gleaming snorting power

Nostrils splayed
In clouds of dust he appears
Shining he appears
Pawing at the air

He dances before her
The colour of the night
Mane tossed like flowing spears of jet
With graceful movement she rises to meet him

Her lord and master, her king and mate.

Jeanette Jackson

COUSINS

They say the cousins should never wed
That a future generation would be too finely bred
But I don't agree with this, you see
As without cousins there wouldn't be me

My mother's aunt was her mother-in-law
Her cousins were her sisters-in-law
Her name didn't change, her name was the same
So if people were confused there was no blame

My parents had a happy life
Though not always free from stress and strife
I was brought up in a loving home
From which I didn't want to roam

My cousin now is my best friend
She always has an ear to lend
So if cousins you know want to marry
Think of me and do not tarry.

Jill Dryden

THE VALUE OF LOVE

If love could be bought,
Would you buy some for me?
Would you value it more,
If love wasn't free?

Would you buy some for birthdays,
And Christmastime too?
And hope someone else,
Will buy some for you.

When you open the box,
You will know love is there,
By the way that your partner,
Has wrapped it with care.

For love is a treasure,
A wonderful gift,
It makes you feel happy,
And gives you a lift.

And if you should get some,
Just spread it around,
For it cannot be bought,
And it cannot be found.

Love has to be given,
By someone who cares,
They don't have to tell you
You'll know when it's there.

By the way they treat you,
And the things that they do,
They don't want to hurt you,
Or make you feel blue.

We all need some love in our life
Don't you think?
Without it, some gamble,
And some turn to drink.

But wherever it comes from,
You'll know when it's there,
By the spring in your step,
When you haven't a care.

When you know that your loved,
It just sets you free,
If you have some to spare,
Would you save it for me?

James Stanley

THINKING, HOPING AND PRAYING

I'm thinking of the lines you wrote
To me from far away
I'm thinking of our dreams and hopes
That mounted day by day.
I'm thinking of you away from me
As times before I've known
I'm thinking of you endlessly
As I sit here all alone.

I'm hoping for success for you
At the dawn of your new day
I'm hoping that your love stays true
And the bonds just won't fray.
I'm hoping for a time to come
When we can really say 'we'
I'm hoping that you're hoping too
To one day be with me.

I'm praying for your happiness
- Your happiness is mine.
I'm praying for your health and strength
To last along the line
I'm praying for inner peace for you
- Your ultimate desire
I'm praying that God will stand with you
To give comfort when you tire.

M V Ward

EQUAL IN LOVE

What we had was divine
Half was hers half was mine.
As I held her hand
I felt a tingle down my spine.
As I looked into her eyes she held back the tears
When near the end after happiness for years.
We had laughed and joked at many a riddle
Not really puzzled we were in the middle.
The time rolled by
Until it was time to say goodbye.
Her memory will be for evermore
A person who I loved and adored.
For as life was on equal term
But for her I still yearn.
I see her face in my memory bank
Her I will always thank.
What she left me is now mine
To cherish for all time.

Allan John Mapstone

NEW GUY

A new guy in town he looks around
For best on the scene hope to stay for a while
To play new games and maybe find his dreams.
Strange lady takes him in gives him a bed and a grin
Just another pretty face a challenge to her base
She wonders where 'he's at' he wonders what's the catch
He thinks she's dumb but she's numb of life's hassles on her scene
He's young and smart, thinks he knows it all
Don't under-estimate her dream
Help each other that's the plan friends are good to know
People take so much from life but never really let go
The timings right it was meant to be, believe in fate and destiny
To share a chapter for a while, see your face begin to smile
Who knows where this story ends maybe lovers or just friends
Woman older than the guy experience she has
Lots of magic in the air makes her want to care
But not to spoil what they have frightened to express
Feelings are so hard to judge in her loneliness
But destiny wins in the end fate you cannot change
Happiness is so free on friends you can depend.

Joyce

IF ONLY

It is not until our soulmate has gone
Who was our other part,
That we really realise what true love is
When no more in a living heart.
If only of your face one more look, one more touch,
Which sadly will never be,
Only in the stillness of a picture
Can you have a look, a touch from me.
We had what seemed a lifetime together
Of laughter but also of tears,
It brought us closer together
To feel as one through all those years.
There was the caring and compassion,
Friendship and love knew no bounds,
Could joke with each other and take no offence
And weathered the ups and the downs.
But now such life is no more.
On ones own times can be tough.
If only one look, one touch once more
But then, it would never be enough.

Tess Walton

IN THE PARK

He took her hand
Her breath
Her will
Her greatest desires.

He found her mouth
Her soul
Her spirit
Her deepest emotions.

He touched her hair
Her core
Her being
Her very life.

He shared his truth
His confusion
His desperation
His passion.

Unfortunately,
His conscience was the only thing
That was pricked!

Milly Shilton

ROOTED

Rooted together in our hearts the sown seed will grow
Then nourished by good laughs, watered by shared tears
This bulb of true friendship will stand true
Against occasional cruel winds of our lives.

Wearing crowns of camaraderie, covered by amaranth flowers
We cuddle and caress, then as problems rain about us
We smile to keep each other safe

Deep in the soil the buds of shared experience
Draw strength from our deep love and respect
Deep underground our intertwined radical roots
Become forever joined

Like Siamese trees
No axe can part us
Friends eternal
In the gardens of love.

C Lee-Rowden

SOULMATES

When you share you soul with someone
It's a hardship just being apart . . .
Your plentiful land is now barren
There's a void of despair in your heart . . .

You reach out to touch your soulmate
And find that there's nobody there . . .
No tender touches of comfort
And no loving aura to share . . .

The company you once took for granted
Has been moved to another zone . . .
Only now do you really understand
The solitude of being alone . . .

These things I write of, have happened to me
And the pain in my heart was intense . . .
But real love knows no barriers
Long distance was only a fence . . .

We may have been physically separated
But our souls were together as one . . .
And the joy of reunification
Was assured, like the dawning sun . . .

I will climb the highest peak on Earth
So that people hear me shout it . . .
Now I've found what true love is
I never want to be without it . . .

Enrico

TOGETHER

Start at the beginning
 Take it nice and slow
Get to know each other
 And let the rest follow

You know the other's name
 You know their favourite song
The nervousness is passing
 I'm sure you'll get along

It's been four weeks now
 Time spent together
Maybe you'll be closer
 Like birds of a feather

Weeks, months - a year
 The future is looking good
Love is growing constantly
 Just like you hoped it would

One day you're getting married
 And now you're husband and wife
Love will conquer everything
 For the rest of your life

Joanne H Hale

LOVE IS . . .

Love is the look upon your face
before each welcoming embrace,
and love is a cup from which we drink
in silence when our bodies link.

Love is a pain within my heart
when time dictates that we must part,
and love is the way you piece my soul
together when I'm not quite whole.

Love is the way your smile destroys
the sadness life sometimes employs,
and love is the beauty in your eyes
where love's deep secret multiplies.

Love is the joy and ecstasy
that reigns within us constantly,
and love is a gift we both can share
along life's busy thoroughfare.

Iaian W Wade

LOVE MADE ME

Gentle goodness that dwells in me
Comforting warmth was Heaven's place of rest
My loving home holds that key

You bestowed such love on us three
Tender soft words, Dearest Mother bless
Gentle goodness that dwells in me

For God's fair hands fashioned thee
You built a strong and cosy nest
My loving home holds that key

Love made me what I am you see
Instilling into me all that's best
Gentle goodness dwells in me

You made me whole then set me free
Carefully edging us towards greatest quest
My loving home holds that key

Preparing, teaching, cajoling, ever constancy
When each day became a teenager's test
Gentle goodness dwells in me
My loving home holds that key.

Ann Hathaway

OH ROMEO

At first she was in silhouette
and then he saw her clear,
working in the fast food store,
the one he held so dear.

Should he approach this vision,
but what words could he say?
He must make this his mission
and not let her get away.

Perhaps she would ignore him,
Oh then his heart would hurt,
but over all the noise and din
she *might* have time to flirt.

Bravely fighting back his fear,
the counter he approached,
to hear those sweet immortal words -
'Scrambled, fried or poached?'

Oh no! This was not his Juliet
(she was on her break)
so he ordered scrambled egg and thought,
what next course could he take?

Whilst sitting at his lonely table,
partaking of his feast,
she reappeared, so sweet, so able,
try again - once more at least.

So he went to order coffee,
and at the counter he did linger,
then all at once he looked, and saw
the ring upon her finger -

Alas, his Juliet was no more!

Ursula J Murray

LONELINESS

I am sitting here, all by myself,
Waiting for the phone to ring
To hear your voice again and again
And to tell you what I think . . . !
I am thinking of the beach,
Our Paradise, our place
And I am praying to God, that you will
Come home safe . . .
I am waiting for a sign from you
I am waiting just to tell you
How much I love you!

Ana Maria Brockie

MY LOVE

How oft my dreams are dreams of you,
How oft my mind you occupy.
Will words express my thoughts untold?
Can written words my tongue untie?

I see you, touch you; hear you,
Smell you, taste you in the sweetest kiss.
Each sense anticipates the way you
Pleasure and take me to a precipice.

I've kissed the salty tears of sorrow
From your cheek; in times of pain.
Have held you close in moments joyous,
Have played the fool; that you would smile again.

Time's drifting veil that dims my eyes,
Life's endless run of day to night.
I've aged; though feelings stay the same,
Love changes meaning; as the flush
Of youth takes flight.

Promises made when we were younger,
When you said 'Yes,' my heart it leapt.
I thank the gods we're still together,
Promises of a lifetime kept.

Should my eyes become unseeing;
Visionless and blind, my hand to tremble;
Confusion wrack my brain,
The face I love more than my life
Would still be etched upon my mind.

K R Turner

A WALK IN THE TREES

I will walk with you among the trees
Tall and straight as they can be
Spruces under, preservation order
No one can touch or harm their bark
Wonderful green, and trunks of brown

Will we my friend grow as old as the trees?
Can we grow as tall, standing side by side?
I can reach out and touch you
Our arms intertwine.
Is that a hint of a smile on your face?

We have known each other just a short time
How can two people be so alike?
It's lovely to walk and take nature in
Just you and me and me and you

As we walk through this wood
May our path never end
Walking through our lives
Together in spirit and mind

I must depart, the day draws in
I will see you soon on the pathway of life.
Now I must go, my friend is calling
Our love is as old as time immemorial
My lover and friend for ever and a day.

New friends will meet, of that I am sure
But my lover is here, it's time to fly
I will tuck you away in my mind till later
We will sit and relax, talk for hours
For now it's just the breeze and I.

Carole A Cleverdon

POSSESSIVENESS

Possessiveness destroys you,
Obsessed with your partner,
Silly obsessions,
Silly worries,
Even to the point of paranoia,
So obsessed it takes over you life,
Someone you can't leave alone,
In an unhealthy way,
Very unhealthy,
Envy and jealousies,
Nuttiness to the point of madness
Everything else forgotten,
Stopping your partner from living,
Stopping yourself from living.

Victoria Dowling

THE LASSO OF LOVE

Love walks behind us every day until we find someone,
Then throws its lasso right away so that the spell's begun!
That's why we linger for a while when really we could leave!
And yet we're captured by a smile with scarcely time to breathe!
Our eyes are drawn as though transfixed, now focused on one face!
At first we stare with feelings mixed, then all falls into place!
Too late! It's happened! There it is; it started with a sigh.
The guy's now pining for a kiss before he says goodbye!
Her eyes are twinkling, yes, they are! Love's lasso then pulls tight!
So that's how come they can't go far! That's why they're so polite!
It's 'Thank you' this and 'Thank you' that and smiles from ear to ear!
He's working hard with all the chat! Yes, something's going on here!
Good God! He's even asked her out! Good God! The girl said, 'Yes!'
Only love could bring this about - that lasso sure can bless!

Denis Martindale

WITHOUT YOU

When day begins
The pink streaked sky
Fills me with wonder and joy
But then my heart turns blue
When I realise that
it will be just another day
- without you -

The day goes on
Places to go
People to meet
So many things to do
But it's still another day
- without you -

Evening comes once again
The darkness all around
Even seems to fill my heart
When I realise that
It will be just another night
- without you -

Oriana Cipriani

THE MISTRESS

Garden weeded and garden seeded,
come with me, my mistress pleaded.
She had a hankering to be seeded too,
to watch a seedling grow anew.

I took her hand, she led me upstairs,
many a time I'd thought of affairs.
I shed my clothes with abandon,
and very soon I had my hands on.

The mistress, the one I adored,
she who couldn't be ignored.
She joked about being fertilised,
how, on my van, my services
could be brightly advertised.

Dan the man,
if he can't fertilise you
nobody can!

Still flowering in her fiftieth year,
that's why I live with the mistress.
Follow her upstairs, do her bidding,
and keep our lovely garden clear.

Danny Coleman

TENDERNESS OF LOVE

Years that bring pleasures
And so many things
Tenderness gentle
As a buttefly's wing
Peace and a haven
From toils of the day
Your lips on mine
While the hours drift away
Night-time till morning
Your heartbeat on mine
Drifting and dreaming
With feelings divine
Magical moments
And years more than most
Life-bringing wishes
And memories and hope.

Jeanette Gaffney

I LOVE YOU

Do you know how much
I love you?
Do you realise how
My heart almost explodes
At the mere mention of
Your name?
And when you're not around
The loneliness
Washes over me
Like a tidal wave
Overwhelming me
And engulfing me and my -
- so-called independence
Leaving me stranded
High and dry
In my not so splendid
Isolation
That's how much I miss you
That's how much I need you
That's how much I love you

Rod Trott

DIANNAH

Riding to hounds, the bugle loud and sharp,
Forest dark and deep, fair Diannah could keep,
the myth of cruelty at bay, as she whittled away,
an hour in her beloved woods.

Where swallows sang in tune,
visitors from Africa, a treasure to see,
Flying in harmony, the stay too brief,
A glorious sight for eyes to feast.

Then riding by came prince and hounds,
he spied the beautiful Diannah,
who was unaware of his intention,
she would be mine to keep.

At first she was exalted,
until she spied the black bear,
who stalked her prince unbeknown,
decided to ensnare.

Diannah turned the prince
with her mystical magical powers
Into a little fox,
the hounds would devour.

The wily little fox
jumped on the back of the bear,
hidden in her black fur,
The hounds would not dare,
Only the occasional sniff and wail,
Told of the hide on the powerful bear
And in due course the prince emerged,
To wed Diannah the fair.

Poor Diannah, simple and naive,
could not imagine the extent of intrigue,
which would engulf her royal status
and destroy her self esteem.
In despair she tried to die,
when all around the critical eye,
was fostered to deny her
a place to breathe and cry.

The hurting was brutal, unrelenting,
unfair to her a honeymoon to share,
with a black fur-coated bear,
always there to pry and stare.

She bore her crush in wealth untold,
in all her riches her misery showed,
eventually to succumb to conspiracy,
a tragic death, where solitude rode.

Atop of poor Diannah,
and there she lies,
not in state but loneliness,
only the birds will cheer her dreams.

Jean Bald

MAIDEN OF DREAMS

Succubus comes to me,
Bestills my heart then offers love.
And so I succumb,
Masonic in her loving touch.
And when she is gone, much missed.

Geoffrey Woodhead

TO LINDA

Is there love in a fleeting glimpse?
A backward glance?
Maybe a second chance?
I've looked briefly into your blue eyes and I've been lost
a thousand times.
The pouting of your lips I long to place upon them the first smouldering
passionate lingering kiss.
I'm attracted to you more today than I can convey it's beyond
comprehension.
I desire you more today than I did yesterday.
The leaves off the trees are falling I feel in my heart of hearts a yearning
for you a distant calling.
Our destinies are entwining, grains in life's hour glass are passing
through grain by grain.
Being without you to my heart there is an emotional strain.
Seeing your face light up with a smile again and again eases my pain.

Jonathan Covington

LEAP YEAR

It is leap year once again
Shall I struggle yet in vain
Will the lads in serviced ranks
With their books from various banks
They must be in the black
Whatever else they lack
I can play the 'Maiden's Prayer',
With a wrong note here and there
I'm not a flower in bud
At sewing I'm a dud
But some have spark
Not one out of the ark
Might take me for a lark
And put me on his knee
And whisper sweet nothings to me
We shall have to wait and see

Miss Fritchley

THE NATURAL WAY

As I think when my arms are around you
The tenderness is more than supple.
Gentleness with your hands too.
My breasts flatten upon the nipple.

A warm smile is given in thought
I feel the circulation of your blood.
Cuddling ends a day that we have fought.
Such an embrace entwines me to be supportive and good!

Heather Edwards

PSYCHOLOGICAL GAMES

With each passing day that goes by
Such moments linger on reflection

We shared so much love and affection
Now we both feel tears of only rejection

No one else knows what's on your mind
You're his human shield he hides behind

I know I have to lose my fear
Hope you survive yet another year

In no more phone calls will I hear you cry
And no more letters we'll write or - reply

You gave me no explanation face to face
And your final letter was such a disgrace

With your moral judgement truly displaced

In your world that's full of pain and blame
His psychological warfare games remain

While you remain irresponsible just the same
God's - not to blame, hang your head in shame.

Graham Hare

STUBBED OUT

For your pleasure only
Deftly rolled, a cigarette
Tobacco in your fingertips
The moment our eyes met

I watched you put it to your lips
And let you taste of mine
You drew enjoyment deeply
As we shared a lover's wine

But smoking is a short-lived joy
And what's of little doubt
You gave me no more thought
Than of the fag that you stubbed out.

Kim Montia

Loss

Bees and kites console me in my losses
What kind of kites,
Do I hear you ask?
Well, they are kind kites, whatever,
Kind and gentle in their comfort,
Caring and comfortable
To those who cry
High-flyers of the air
Bright shiners
And their eyes
Are gentle.

The bees, like besoms, sweep the rubbish out
From hives where new life seethes.
They burr and bumble
On each lucid pane
Where they are shown to curious eyes of children.
Their drowsy murmurings
The summer long prolong
Our dream of happiness
Daydreams in meadows of long grass
Or idly upon a dhooli slowly swinging
While all around us little signs of life
Are swelling.

Kind eyes and droning bees
Attendant on my pain
Hear all my groaning grieving,
Demand
No instant answer

Offer
No easy consolations
Around the yawning grave, the
Widening wound of emptiness
That grows more painful daily
Quietly continue only to be there
With their light touch refraining
From entering where
No angel dare.

Bees droning in my bonnet;
Kites flying high within my skull;
At night I try to snatch at them,
To catch them as I can:
For so in taming these stray wanderers
And giving them a hive to honey in,
A nest to nurture in,
A verse is made, a rhythm and a hum
Contentedness can nestle in;
And sorrow sing.

Joan Kirby

MY LOVE FOR YOU

My love for you is so very strong
Without you I just couldn't go on
Your merest glance, your slightest smile
You make my poor heart leap a mile

My love for you is so very strong
How did I survive without you for so long?
Upon hearing the crushed velvet of your voice
I realise I just didn't have a choice (but to love you)

My love for you is so very strong
Can these intense emotions be so wrong
You most loving hug, your most sweetest kiss
Oh what a wonderful moment of bliss

My love for you is so very strong
At last I know where I belong
So my darling please stay by my side
And by love's rules I will abide

Jacqueline Hailes

CLOSE ENCOUNTERS

There are not many times I've truly loved,
Or been loved the same in return,
Loving relationships transient proved,
Plunging headlong, will never learn.

Minds and bodies join, not counting the cost,
Joy when my love and I are one,
Having blindly pursued, all reason lost,
Until love has flown and is gone.

As doubts creep in, a voice of warning sounds,
Love can never stay the distance;
Retreat into corners, love out of bounds,
Pretend it's of no importance?

But truth cannot be hidden from the heart
While inside aching with longing,
Agony of breaking up, tears still smart,
What choice is left but belonging?

Once, awoke with feelings of happiness,
Dreaming my lover still loved me,
Soon knew it was but a dream, then sadness,
Dreams are never meant to be.

Our thoughts for a while were deeply entwined,
I always believed it would last,
Many a time I've wanted to remind
Of shared memories of the past.

Gazing long at one another, what bliss,
Two souls joined though bodies apart,
Is it not better to know love like this
Than to end with a broken heart?

Betty Mealand

Wow

Their eyes met across a crowded room,
they'd been watching each other all night.
They walked across the dancing floor
and met beneath the disco light.

He places one hand upon her back
and the other in her right hand.
They began to shuffle around the floor
and he carefully eyed the band.

She suddenly stopped to look at him
and he hung his head to the floor.
He wished that she would trip and fall,
so he could run out of the door.

She lifted his chin up to her level
and he tried to avert his eyes.
She asked him what was wrong
and he told a tiny lie.

She wrapped her arms around his neck
and pulled him in towards her.
Their lips just slightly brushed
and she pulled him even closer.

Suddenly his eyes flicker open
and he looked around the room
'Wow!' I wish I could have more dreams like that,
cos that one was boom!'

Emily Ruth Henderson (15)

LET DOWN

'Leave him come and live with me,'
You said it every day.
'We're meant to be together
In every kind of way.

You fill my life, I love you,'
You often said to me.
'So leave your man immediately
And come and live with me.'

'But you have got a wife,' I said
'And you will never leave
She needs your presence in the home
And you know you are weak.'

'Oh no I can do it,'
You often said to me.
'So leave your man immediately
And come and live with me.'

And after many episodes
Of begging me to go
I left my man to be with you
But you just couldn't go.

And when I said to you, 'What now?
You've left me in a mess.'
'You knew I couldn't do it,' you said.
What more could I expect?

Denise Tidswell

ALTERNATIVE DREAM

The single whisper
Of lonely hearts,
That tender touch
Of softest hands.

Silently prevails
Beyond my grasp
Night is cold -
The moon is black.

The deepest fear
Of losing you,
Can't stay still,
My eyes cry closed.

Heikki Loimulahti

INNOCUOUS BEGINNINGS

Innocuous beginnings
It relies on chance
A few casual words
Exchanged or a glance

But from these moments
Love steadily grows
Auditioning its part
Then stealing the show

Alan Wilson

SUMMER DREAMING

One night I dreamt a perfect dream,
in which you shared my everything,
my world you had in your hand
and you held me tight in the summer sand
my happiness you kept alive
and laughter filled my every stride.

Then I woke one summer day,
when my eyes were filled with golden rays,
and I saw you sleeping by my side
protecting me like a golden tide,
that washes away all fears and tears,
for now I realise my perfect dream
but was a true life story told.

Claire Holsey

GONE FOR EVER

Forget his name,
Forget his face,
Forget his kiss, his warm embrace,
Forget the love you once knew,
Remember he's with someone new,
Forget him when they play your song,
Forget you cried all night long,
Forget how close you two once were,
Remember he has chosen her,
Forget his laugh,
Forget his grin,
Forget his dimple on his chin,
Forget the way he held you tight,
Remember he's with her tonight,.
Forget the love that went so fast,
Forget he said he'd leave you never,
Remember now he's gone for ever.

L McPhee

LOVE IS LIKE A GAME

When at first we fall in love
We close our eyes
and the world felt it has just closed up
Our hearts and minds they think alike
they put up a shield
that locks the world out
For we don't see those around us
we're so much in love with our new finding
we don't want to let go
for our bodies are binding.

A Houghton

DREAM LOVER

I gently close my eyes and slip into a special place,
Lined with beautiful pink and white trees, moving with grace.
There is no noise and no frightening things,
For I am in a wonderful land that joy and happiness brings.
Out from the trees appears this angel-like figure.
Everything about her so elegant, it sends me to shiver.
This lady walks over on the floor of golden sand,
She calls out my name, and holds out her hand,
She takes my palm and places it on her heart,
Then whispers softly, 'We'll never be apart,'
My body is talking and telling her eyes,
I am feeling something special and joyful inside,
Something stirs me, I wake and turn to my side,
She is there before me, a tear is wept, my emotions can't hide.
The special, surreal land I have just left,
I have been a part of since the day we first met.
So my land of dreams is already complete,
And it does not matter if I am awake or asleep.

R A Shepherd

THE PARTING

You said you'd never leave me
Be always by my side
Your hand be there to guide me
To a place where I could hide
When the world was full of darkness
And the sun was lost in cloud
Your arms would close around me
And your strength would make me proud
Would give me hope and courage
To face the storm once more
Knowing that your love was certain
And my future was secure
Then came the day when time stood still
The told me you were gone from here
My life, your love no more would fill
I lost my strength, my hope, my will
But time goes by and life goes on
The pain is less, the tears have dried
A p art of me is missing now
It went with you the day you died.

A Wheeler

I SIT ALONE

I sit alone
Wondering
Believing you would come
You're in my mind
I'm all mixed up
In pain
And grief
I hear your footsteps
But you don't come
I sit alone and remember
Your smell
Your rough touch
Your love
You gave so much
But received so little
I sit alone
But you're with me.

Donna Moulding

BROKEN PROMISES

You don't keep promises anymore,
Yet you say I'm the one you adore,
You, I can no longer fight,
You always end up being right.

Why promises to me you always break,
How much more do you think I can take,
You say to you I come first,
But this only makes matter worse.

Things go wrong with all we planned,
This is something I don't understand,
So often about these things we talk,
I must be thick, I can't tell cheese from chalk.

Often I feel like walking away,
But at the back I always stay.
It's hard to follow in your track.
There must be something that I lack.

I see the past every time I dream,
You say things are not what they seem.
Are promises a good game to play?
Only used when you cannot stay.

Broken promises keep two apart,
May cause a weakening of the heart.
A weakened heart soon will break,
When no more broken promises can it take.

Margaret Upson

SUBMISSIONS INVITED
SOMETHING FOR EVERYONE

POETRY NOW 2002 - Any subject,
any style, any time.

WOMENSWORDS 2002 - Strictly women,
have your say the female way!

STRONGWORDS 2002 - Warning!
Age restriction, must be between 16-24,
opinionated and have strong views.
(Not for the faint-hearted)

All poems no longer than 30 lines.
Always welcome! No fee!
Cash Prizes to be won!

Mark your envelope (eg *Poetry Now) 2002*
Send to:
Forward Press Ltd
Remus House, Coltsfoot Drive,
Peterborough, PE2 9JX

**OVER £10,000 POETRY PRIZES
TO BE WON!**

Judging will take place in October 2002